Practical
Chocolate

p^3

This is a P³ Book
This edition published in 2003

P³
Queen Street House
4 Queen Street
Bath BA1 1HE, UK

ISBN: 1-40542-306-4

Manufactured in China

NOTE

Cup measurements in this book are for American cups.
This book also uses imperial and metric measurements. Follow the same units
of measurement throughout; do not mix imperial and metric.
All spoon measurements are level: teaspoons are assumed to be 5 ml, and
tablespoons are assumed to be 15 ml. Unless otherwise stated,
milk is assumed to be whole milk, eggs and individual vegetables such as potatoes
are medium, and pepper is freshly ground black pepper.

The nutritional information provided for each recipe is per serving or per person.
Optional ingredients, variations, or serving suggestions have
not been included in the calculations. The times given for each recipe are an approximate
guide only because the preparation times may differ according to the techniques used by
different people and the cooking times may vary as a result of the type of oven used.

Recipes using raw or very lightly cooked eggs should be
avoided by infants, the elderly, pregnant women, convalescents,
and anyone suffering from an illness.

Contents

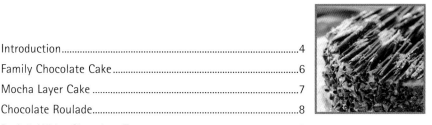

Introduction

Chocolate!—even the word is an enticing mixture of indulgence tinged with a touch of sinfulness, and the product itself more than lives up to its promise. The mere mention of anything associated with this mouthwatering confection can cause a dreamy look to come into the eyes of the chocoholic. Over the centuries it has even been regarded as an aphrodisiac. Chocolate actually melts at body temperature, which is probably why it has always been regarded as such a sensual food. Whether or not it can liven up your love-life, however, there is no doubt that chocolate is adored by everyone.

The cocoa tree, *Theobroma cacao*, originated in South America, and from the early 7th century it was cultivated by the Maya, who established a flourishing trade and even used the cocoa bean as currency. In 1502, Christopher Columbus took the cocoa bean to Spain, but it wasn't until later that Cortés introduced *xocolatl*, a recipe brought from the Mexican court of Montezuma for a drink made from crushed roasted cocoa beans and cold water, thickened with cornstarch and frothed with a swizzle stick. Vanilla, spices, honey, and sugar were added to improve the flavor of this thick and bitter brew, and over time it came to be served hot. Cocoa was believed to cure a variety of physical illnesses and to promote stamina.

In the 17th century, the popularity of cocoa spread to the rest of Europe. France was the first country to fall to its charms, then Holland, where Amsterdam became the most important cocoa port beyond Spain. From there cocoa went to Germany, then north to Scandinavia, and also south to Italy—by which time it had become a major source of revenue.

Cocoa arrived in England in the mid 17th century, and chocolate houses quickly began to rival the newly established coffee houses.

In the early 19th century, Dutch chemist Coenraad Van Houten invented a press to extract the fat from the beans, and developed a method of neutralizing the acids. In this way, he was able to produce

almost pure cocoa butter, and a hard "cake," which could be milled to a powder for use as a flavoring. As a result, it became possible to eat chocolate as well as to drink it.

It was soon discovered that the rich cocoa butter made a delicious confection, and chocolate production began in earnest. In Britain, Fry's chocolate appeared in 1847, and in Switzerland the famous chocolate companies were established. In 1875 chocolate was combined with condensed milk to produce the first milk

chocolate. At around this time, Lindt found a way of making the smooth, melting chocolate still associated with his company today. About 20 years later, Hershey introduced his famous chocolate bar in the United States, where chocolate is perhaps better loved than anywhere else.

Today, cocoa trees are grown in Africa, the West Indies, the tropical areas of America, and the Far East. Harvested cocoa beans are left in the heat of the sun to develop their chocolate flavor, then afterward the beans are shelled, and the kernels are processed to produce cocoa solids. Finally, the cocoa butter is extracted and processed again to become chocolate, in all its many guises.

Preparing chocolate

To melt chocolate on a stove:

1 Break the chocolate into small, equal-size pieces and put it into a heatproof bowl.

2 Place the bowl over a pan of hot, simmering water, making sure the bottom of the bowl does not come into contact with the water.

3 Once the chocolate starts to melt, stir gently until smooth, then remove from the heat.

Note: do not melt chocolate over direct heat (unless melting with other ingredients—in this case, keep the heat very low).

To melt chocolate in a microwave oven:

1 Break chocolate into small pieces and place in a microwave-proof bowl.

2 Put the bowl in the microwave oven and melt. As a guide, melt 4½ oz/125 g dark chocolate on HIGH for 2 minutes, and white or milk chocolate on MEDIUM for 2–3 minutes.

Note: microwave oven temperatures and settings vary, so you should consult the manufacturer's instructions first.

3 Stir the chocolate, let stand for a few minutes, then stir again. If necessary, return it to the microwave for 30 seconds more.

Chocolate decorations

Decorations add a special touch to a cake or dessert. They can be interleaved with nonstick baking parchment and stored in airtight containers. Dark chocolate will keep for 4 weeks, and milk or white chocolate for 2 weeks.

Caraque

1 Melt a quantity of chocolate as described above, then quickly spread it over a clean acrylic cutting board and let set until firm.

2 When the chocolate has set, hold the board firmly, position a large, smooth-bladed knife on the chocolate, and pull the blade toward you at an angle of 45 degrees, scraping along the chocolate to form the caraque. You should end up with irregularly shaped long curls (see right).

3 Using the knife blade, lift the caraque off the board and use it for decoration as required.

Quick curls

1 For quick curls, choose a thick bar of chocolate and keep it at room temperature.

2 Using a sharp, swivel-bladed vegetable peeler, scrape lightly along the chocolate to form fine curls, or more firmly to form thicker curls.

Leaves

1 Use freshly picked leaves with well-defined veins that are clean, dry, and pliable. Holding a leaf by its stem, paint a smooth layer of melted chocolate onto the underside with a small paint brush or pastry brush.

2 Repeat with the remaining leaves, then place them, chocolate side up, on a cookie sheet lined with waxed paper.

3 Refrigerate for at least an hour until set. When set, peel each leaf away from its chocolate coating.

KEY	
Simplicity level 1–3 (1 easiest, 3 slightly harder)	
Preparation time	
Cooking time	

Family Chocolate Cake

A simple-to-make family cake ideal for an everyday treat. Keep the decoration simple—you could use a store-bought frosting or filling, if liked.

1 hr   20 mins

SERVES 8

INGREDIENTS

½ cup soft margarine, plus extra for greasing

½ cup superfine sugar

2 eggs

1 tbsp light corn syrup

1 cup self-rising flour, sifted

2 tbsp unsweetened cocoa, sifted

FILLING AND TOPPING

4 tbsp confectioners' sugar, sifted

2 tbsp butter

3½ oz/100 g white or light cooking chocolate

a little light or white chocolate, melted (optional)

1 Lightly grease two 7-inch/18-cm shallow cake pans.

2 Place all of the ingredients for the cake in a large mixing bowl and beat with a wooden spoon or electric hand whisk to form a smooth mixture.

3 Divide the mixture between the prepared pans and level the tops. Bake in a preheated oven, 375°F/190°C, for 20 minutes, or until springy to the touch. Cool for a few minutes in the pans before transferring to a wire rack to cool completely.

4 To make the filling, beat the confectioners' sugar and butter together in a bowl until light and fluffy.

Melt the cooking chocolate and beat half into the filling. Use the filling to sandwich the 2 cakes together.

5 Spread the remaining melted cooking chocolate over the top of the cake. Pipe circles of contrasting melted light or white chocolate and feather into the cooking chocolate with a toothpick, if desired. Let the cake set before serving.

COOK'S TIP

Ensure that you eat this cake on the day of baking because it does not keep well.

Mocha Layer Cake

Chocolate cake and a creamy coffee-flavored filling are combined in this delicious mocha cake.

50 mins

35–45 mins

SERVES 8

I N G R E D I E N T S

1 tbsp butter, for greasing

1¾ cups self-rising flour

¼ tsp baking powder

4 tbsp unsweetened cocoa

½ cup superfine sugar

2 eggs

2 tbsp light corn syrup

⅔ cup sunflower oil

⅔ cup milk

F I L L I N G

1 tsp instant coffee powder

1 tbsp boiling water

1¼ cups heavy cream

2 tbsp confectioners' sugar

T O   D E C O R A T E

1¾ oz/50 g flock or flaked chocolate

chocolate caraque (see page 5)

confectioners' sugar, to dust

1 Lightly grease three 7-inch/18-cm cake pans.

2 Sift the flour, baking powder, and cocoa into a large mixing bowl. Stir in the sugar. Make a well in the center and stir in the eggs, corn syrup, oil, and milk. Beat with a wooden spoon, gradually mixing in the dry ingredients to make a smooth batter. Divide the mixture between the prepared pans.

3 Bake in a preheated oven, 350°F/ 180°C, for 35–45 minutes, or until springy to the touch. Let cool in the pans for 5 minutes, then turn out onto a wire rack to cool completely.

4 Dissolve the instant coffee in the boiling water and place in a bowl with the cream and confectioners' sugar. Whip until the cream is just holding its shape. Use half of the cream to sandwich the 3 cakes together. Spread the remaining cream over the top and sides of the cake. Lightly press the flock or flaked chocolate into the cream around the edge of the cake.

5 Transfer to a serving plate. Lay the caraque over the top of the cake. Cut a few thin strips of baking parchment and place on top of the caraque. Dust lightly with confectioners' sugar, then carefully remove the paper. Serve.

Chocolate Roulade

Don't worry if the cake cracks when rolled, this is quite normal. If it doesn't crack, consider yourself a real chocolate wizard in the kitchen!

🍰 1 hr   🕐 12 mins

SERVES 6

INGREDIENTS

5½ oz/150 g dark chocolate

2 tbsp water

6 eggs

¾ cup superfine sugar

¼ cup all-purpose flour

1 tbsp unsweetened cocoa

FILLING

1¼ cups heavy cream

2¾ oz/75 g sliced strawberries

TO DECORATE

confectioners' sugar, plus extra for dusting

chocolate leaves (see page 5)

1 Line a 15 x 10-inch/37.5 x 25-cm jelly roll pan. Melt the chocolate in the water, stirring. Let cool slightly.

2 Place the eggs and sugar in a bowl and whisk for 10 minutes, or until the mixture is pale and foamy and the whisk leaves a trail when lifted. Whisk in the chocolate in a thin stream. Sift the flour and cocoa together and fold into the mixture. Pour into the pan; level the top.

3 Bake in a preheated oven, 400°F/ 200°C, for 12 minutes. Dust a sheet of baking parchment with a little confectioners' sugar. Turn out the roulade and remove the lining paper. Roll up the roulade with the fresh parchment inside. Place on a wire rack, cover with a damp dish towel, and let cool.

4 Whisk the cream. Unroll the roulade and scatter over the fruit. Spread three-fourths of the cream over the roulade and re-roll. Dust the roulade with confectioners' sugar.

5 Place the roulade on a plate. Pipe the rest of the cream down the center. Make the chocolate leaves (see page 5) and use them to decorate the roulade.

Dark & White Chocolate Torte

If you can't decide if you prefer bitter dark chocolate or rich creamy white chocolate, then this gateau is for you.

🍰 🍰 🍰

🍰 1 hr 5 mins ⏱ 35–40 mins

SERVES 6

INGREDIENTS

1 tbsp butter, for greasing

4 eggs

½ cup superfine sugar

¾ cup all-purpose flour

DARK CHOCOLATE CREAM

⅔ cup heavy cream

5½ oz/150 g dark chocolate

WHITE CHOCOLATE FROSTING

2¾ oz/75 g white chocolate

1 tbsp butter

1 tbsp milk

4 tbsp confectioners' sugar

chocolate caraque (see page 5)

1 Grease an 8-inch/20-cm round springform pan and line the bottom. Beat the eggs and superfine sugar in a large mixing bowl with an electric whisk or hand whisk for about 10 minutes, or until the mixture is very light and foamy and the whisk leaves a trail that lasts a few seconds when lifted.

2 Sift the flour and fold in with a metal spoon or spatula. Pour into the prepared pan and bake in a preheated oven, 350°F/180°C, for 35–40 minutes, or until springy to the touch. Let the cake cool slightly, then transfer to a wire rack to cool completely.

3 While the cake is cooling, make the chocolate cream. Place the cream in a pan and bring to a boil, stirring. Break the dark chocolate into small pieces and stir into the cream until melted. Pour the mixture into a heatproof bowl and let cool. Beat with a wooden spoon until thick.

4 Cut the cold cake into 2 layers horizontally. Sandwich the layers back together with the chocolate cream and place on a wire rack.

5 To make the frosting, melt the white chocolate and butter together and stir until blended. Whisk in the milk and confectioners' sugar, and continue whisking until cool. Pour over the cake and spread with a spatula to coat the top and sides. Decorate with chocolate caraque and let the frosting set.

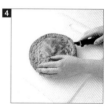

Chocolate Fruit Loaf

A very moreish loaf that smells divine while it is cooking.
This loaf is best eaten warm.

1 hr 40 mins   30 mins

SERVES 10

I N G R E D I E N T S

2 tbsp butter, melted, plus extra for greasing

3 cups white bread flour

¼ cup unsweetened cocoa

2 tbsp superfine sugar

6 g sachet rapid-rise dry yeast

¼ tsp salt

1 cup lukewarm water

5 tbsp roughly chopped candied cherries

½ cup dark chocolate chips

⅓ cup golden raisins

2¾ oz/75 g no-soak dried apricots,
   coarsely chopped

G L A Z E

1 tbsp superfine sugar

1 tbsp water

1 Lightly grease a 2-lb/900-g loaf pan. Sift the flour and cocoa into a large mixing bowl. Stir in the sugar, dry yeast, and salt.

2 Mix together the lukewarm water and remaining butter. Make a well in the center of the dry ingredients and add the liquid. Mix well with a wooden spoon, then use your hands to bring the dough together. Turn out onto a lightly floured counter and knead for 5 minutes, until a smooth elastic dough forms. Return to a clean bowl, cover with a damp dish towel, and let rise in a warm place for about 1 hour or until doubled in size.

3 Turn the dough out onto a floured counter and knead for 5 minutes. Roll out to a rectangle about ½ inch/1 cm thick and the same width as the length of the pan. Scatter the cherries, chocolate chips, golden raisins, and chopped apricots over the dough. Carefully roll up the dough, like a jelly roll, enclosing the filling. Transfer to the loaf pan, cover with a damp dish towel, and let rise for about 20 minutes, or until the top of the dough is level with the top of the pan.

4 To make the glaze, mix together the sugar and water, then brush it over the top of the loaf. Bake in a preheated oven, 400°F/200°C, for 30 minutes, or until well risen. Serve.

Chocolate Bread

For the chocoholics among us, this bread is great fun to make and even better to eat.

2 hrs   25–30 mins

MAKES 1 LOAF

INGREDIENTS

1 tbsp butter, for greasing

4 cups white bread flour

¼ cup unsweetened cocoa

1 tsp salt

1 sachet rapid-rise dry yeast

2 tbsp soft brown sugar

1 tbsp oil

1¼ cups lukewarm water

1 Lightly grease a 2-lb/900-g loaf pan with butter.

2 Sift the flour and cocoa into a large mixing bowl.

3 Stir in the salt, dry yeast, and soft brown sugar.

4 Pour in the oil along with the lukewarm water and mix the ingredients together to make a dough.

5 Place the dough on a lightly floured counter and knead for 5 minutes.

6 Place the dough in a greased bowl, cover, and let rise in a warm place for about 1 hour, or until the dough has doubled in size.

7 Punch down the dough and shape it into a loaf. Place the dough in the prepared pan, cover, and let rise in a warm place for another 30 minutes.

8 Bake in a preheated oven, 400°F/200°C, for 25–30 minutes, or until a hollow sound is heard when the bottom of the bread is tapped.

9 Transfer the bread to a wire rack and let cool. Cut into slices to serve.

COOK'S TIP
This bread can be sliced and spread with butter or it can be lightly toasted.

Mini Chocolate Gingers

Individually made desserts look professional and are quick to cook. If you do not have small ovenproof bowls, use small teacups instead.

20 mins

45 mins

SERVES 4

INGREDIENTS

generous ⅓ cup soft margarine, plus extra for greasing

¾ cup self-rising flour, sifted

½ cup superfine sugar

2 eggs

¼ cup unsweetened cocoa, sifted

1 oz/25 g dark chocolate

1¾ oz/50 g preserved ginger

CHOCOLATE CUSTARD

2 egg yolks

1 tbsp superfine sugar

1 tbsp cornstarch

1¼ cups milk

3½ oz/100 g dark chocolate, broken into pieces

confectioners' sugar, to dust

1 Lightly grease 4 small individual ovenproof bowls. Place the margarine, flour, sugar, eggs, and cocoa in a mixing bowl and beat until well combined and smooth. Chop the chocolate and ginger and stir into the mixture.

2 Spoon the cake mixture into the prepared bowls and level the tops. The mixture should three-fourths fill the bowls. Cover the bowls with disks of baking parchment and cover with pleated sheets of aluminum foil. Steam for about 45 minutes, until the sponges are cooked and springy to the touch.

3 Meanwhile, make the custard. Beat together the egg yolks, sugar, and cornstarch to form a smooth paste. Heat the milk until boiling and whisk into the egg mixture. Return to the pan and cook over very low heat, stirring, until thick. Remove from the heat and beat in the chocolate. Stir until the chocolate melts.

4 Lift the mini chocolate gingers from the steamer, run a knife around the edge of the bowls, and turn out onto serving plates. Dust with sugar and drizzle chocolate custard over the top. Serve the remaining custard separately.

Chocolate Fudge Dessert

This fabulous steamed sponge, served with a rich chocolate fudge sauce, is perfect for cold winter days.

10 mins   1½–2 hrs

SERVES 6

INGREDIENTS

generous ⅓ cup soft margarine, plus extra for greasing

1¼ cups self-rising flour

½ cup light corn syrup

3 eggs

¼ cup unsweetened cocoa

CHOCOLATE FUDGE SAUCE

3½ oz/100 g dark chocolate

½ cup condensed milk

4 tbsp heavy cream

1 Lightly grease a 5-cup/1.2-liter heatproof bowl.

2 Place the ingredients for the sponge in a separate mixing bowl and beat until well combined and smooth.

3 Spoon into the prepared bowl and level the top. Cover with a disk of waxed paper and tie a pleated sheet of aluminum foil over the bowl. Steam for 1½–2 hours, until cooked and springy to the touch.

4 To make the sauce, break the chocolate into small pieces and place in a small pan with the condensed milk. Heat gently, stirring, until the chocolate melts.

5 Remove the pan from the heat and stir in the heavy cream.

6 To serve the dessert, turn it out onto a serving plate and pour over a little of the chocolate fudge sauce. Serve the remaining sauce separately.

Chocolate Meringue Pie

Crumbly cracker bottom, rich creamy chocolate filling topped with fluffy meringue—what could be more indulgent than this fabulous dessert?

25 mins   35 mins

SERVES 6

INGREDIENTS

8 oz/225 g dark chocolate graham crackers

4 tbsp butter

FILLING

3 egg yolks

4 tbsp superfine sugar

4 tbsp cornstarch

2½ cups milk

3½ oz/100 g dark chocolate, melted

MERINGUE

2 egg whites

½ cup superfine sugar

¼ tsp vanilla extract

1   Place the graham crackers in a plastic bag and crush with a rolling pin. Pour into a mixing bowl. Melt the butter and stir it into the cracker crumbs until well mixed. Press the graham cracker mixture firmly into the bottom and up the sides of a 9-inch/23-cm tart pan or dish.

2   To make the filling, beat the egg yolks, superfine sugar, and cornstarch in a large bowl until they form a smooth paste, adding a little of the milk if necessary. Heat the milk until almost boiling, then slowly pour it onto the egg mixture, whisking well.

3   Return the mixture to the pan and cook gently, whisking constantly, until it thickens. Remove from the heat. Whisk in the melted chocolate, then pour it onto the graham cracker pie shell.

4   To make the meringue, place the egg whites in a large mixing bowl and whisk well, until standing in soft peaks. Gradually whisk in about two-thirds of the sugar, until the mixture is stiff and glossy. Fold in the remaining sugar and the vanilla extract.

5   Spread the meringue over the filling, swirling the surface with the back of a spoon to give it an attractive finish. Bake in the center of a preheated oven, 375°F/190°C, for 30 minutes, or until the meringue is golden. Serve the pie hot or just warm.

Chocolate Fondue

This is a fun dessert to serve at the end of a meal. Prepare in advance, then simply warm through before serving.

10 mins   5 mins

SERVES 4

INGREDIENTS

8 oz/225 g dark chocolate

generous ¾ cup heavy cream

2 tbsp brandy

TO SERVE

selection of fruit

white and pink marshmallows

sweet cookies

1 Break the chocolate into small pieces and place in a small pan with the heavy cream.

2 Heat the mixture gently, stirring constantly, until the chocolate has melted and blended with the cream.

3 Remove the pan from the heat and stir in the brandy.

4 Pour into a fondue pot or a small flameproof dish and keep warm, preferably over a small burner.

5 Serve with a selection of fruit, marshmallows, and cookies for dipping. The fruit and marshmallows can be spiked on fondue forks, wooden skewers, or ordinary forks, for dipping into the chocolate fondue.

COOK'S TIP

To prepare the fruit for dipping, cut larger fruit into bite-size pieces. Fruits that discolor, such as bananas, apples, and pears, should be dipped in a little lemon juice as soon as they are cut.

Hot Chocolate Soufflé

Served with hot chocolate custard, this is a chocoholic's dream. Do not be put off by the mystique of soufflés—this one is not difficult to make.

15 mins   50–55 mins

SERVES 4

INGREDIENTS

2 tbsp butter, plus extra for greasing

3½ oz/100 g dark chocolate

1¼ cups milk

4 large eggs, separated

1 tbsp cornstarch

4 tbsp superfine sugar

½ tsp vanilla extract

⅔ cup dark chocolate chips

superfine and confectioners' sugar, to dust

CHOCOLATE CUSTARD

2 tbsp cornstarch

1 tbsp superfine sugar

scant 2 cups milk

1¾ oz/50 g dark chocolate

1 Grease a 5-cup soufflé dish and sprinkle with superfine sugar. Break the dark chocolate into pieces.

2 Heat the milk with the butter in a pan until almost boiling. Mix the egg yolks, cornstarch, and 4 tablespoons of superfine sugar in a bowl and pour on some of the hot milk, whisking. Return it to the pan and cook gently, stirring constantly, until thickened. Add the chocolate and stir until melted. Remove from the heat and stir in the vanilla extract.

3 Whisk the egg whites until standing in soft peaks. Fold half of the egg whites into the chocolate mixture. Fold in the rest with the chocolate chips. Pour into the dish and bake in a preheated oven, 350°F/180°C, for 40–45 minutes, until well risen.

4 Meanwhile, make the custard. Put the cornstarch and superfine sugar in a small bowl and mix to a smooth paste with a little of the milk. Heat the remaining milk until almost boiling. Pour a little of the hot milk onto the cornstarch, mix well, then pour back into the pan. Cook gently, stirring, until thickened. Break the chocolate into pieces and add to the custard, stirring, until melted.

5 Dust the soufflé with confectioners' sugar and serve immediately with the chocolate custard.

Chocolate Ravioli

Tempting squares of homemade chocolate pasta are filled with a mouthwatering mixture of mascarpone cheese and white chocolate.

25 mins, plus 1 hr chilling/resting   10 mins

SERVES 4

INGREDIENTS

1½ cups all-purpose flour, plus 2 tbsp extra for dusting

4 tbsp unsweetened cocoa

2 tbsp confectioners' sugar

2 eggs, lightly beaten, plus extra for brushing

1 tbsp vegetable oil

FILLING

6 oz/175 g white chocolate, broken into pieces

1 cup mascarpone cheese

1 egg

1 tbsp finely chopped preserved ginger

fresh mint sprigs, to decorate

heavy cream, to serve

1 Sift together the flour, cocoa, and sugar onto a clean counter. Make a well in the center and pour the 2 beaten eggs and the oil into it. Gradually draw in the flour with your fingertips, until it is fully incorporated. Alternatively, sift the flour, cocoa, and sugar into a food processor, add the eggs and oil, and process until mixed. Knead the dough until it is smooth and elastic, then cover with plastic wrap and place in the refrigerator for 30 minutes to chill.

2 Meanwhile, to make the filling, put the white chocolate in the top of a double boiler or in a heatproof bowl set over a pan of barely simmering water. When the chocolate has melted, remove it from the heat and cool slightly, then beat in the mascarpone and the egg. Stir in the chopped ginger.

3 Remove the pasta dough from the refrigerator, cut it in half and keep one half tightly wrapped in plastic wrap. Roll out the first half of the dough into a rectangle on a lightly floured counter, then cover with a clean, damp dish towel. Roll out the other half into a rectangle. Spoon the chocolate and ginger filling into a pastry bag and pipe small mounds in even rows at intervals of about 1½ inches/4 cm over 1 dough rectangle. Brush the spaces between the mounds with beaten egg, then, using a rolling pin to lift it, position the second dough rectangle on top of the first. Press firmly between the mounds with your finger to seal and push out any pockets of air. Cut the dough into squares around the mounds using a serrated ravioli or dough cutter or a sharp knife. Transfer the ravioli to a lightly floured dish towel and let rest for 30 minutes.

4 Bring a large pan of water to a boil, then lower the heat to medium and cook the ravioli, in batches, stirring to prevent them from sticking together, for 4–5 minutes, until tender but still firm to the bite. Remove with a slotted spoon. Serve immediately on individual plates, garnished with mint sprigs, and hand the cream separately.

Nut & Chocolate Pasta

This is a popular entrée in northern Europe, and it also makes a satisfying vegetarian supper.

20 mins

35–40 mins

SERVES 4

I N G R E D I E N T S

salt

12 oz/350 g dried ribbon pasta, such as
tagliatelle or fettuccine

1 tsp butter, for greasing

2–3 tbsp fresh white bread crumbs

S A U C E

6 tbsp butter

¾ cup confectioners' sugar

4 eggs, separated

¾ cup ground, roasted hazelnuts

3 oz/85 g dark chocolate, grated

4 tbsp fresh white bread crumbs

½ tsp ground cinnamon

zest of ½ lemon, finely grated

1 Bring a large pan of lightly salted water to a boil. Add the pasta and cook for 6 minutes or according to the instructions on the package, until tender but still firm to the bite. Drain, rinse under cold running water, and set aside.

2 To make the sauce, beat together the butter, half the confectioners' sugar, and the egg yolks, until frothy.

3 Put the egg whites in a separate bowl with the remaining confectioners' sugar and whisk together until stiff, then fold them into the butter mixture.

4 In another bowl, mix the hazelnuts, grated chocolate, bread crumbs, cinnamon, and lemon zest, then stir into the egg mixture. Add the pasta and stir gently to mix.

5 Preheat the oven to 400°F/200°C. Grease an ovenproof dish with butter and sprinkle with bread crumbs. Tap lightly to coat the bottom and sides, then tip out any excess. Spoon the pasta mixture into the dish and bake in the preheated oven for 25–30 minutes. Serve immediately, with roasted vine tomatoes (see Cook's Tip), if desired.

COOK'S TIP
To roast vine tomatoes, put 12 small tomatoes in an oven-proof dish, then sprinkle over about 2 tablespoons of olive oil, and season with salt and pepper to taste. Roast in an oven preheated to 400°F/200°C for 15–20 minutes, then remove from the oven and serve hot.

Veal in Chocolate Sauce

Chocolate can enrich stews based on a broad range of meats, including game, but it is important to be light-handed or it can become cloying.

🐷 🐷 🐷

🥘 20 mins 🕐 1¾ hrs

SERVES 4

INGREDIENTS

5 tbsp vegetable oil

1 lb 8 oz/675 g boneless veal (or pork if veal is unavailable), cut into 1-inch/2.5-cm cubes

1 onion, chopped

2 garlic cloves, chopped

2 carrots, chopped

2 celery stalks, chopped

2 fresh red chiles, seeded and chopped

1¼–1¾ cups red wine

½ cup beef bouillon

2 tsp chopped fresh thyme

1 bay leaf

4 juniper berries, lightly crushed

2 cloves

1-inch/2.5-cm piece of cinnamon stick

8 oz/225 g chestnuts

8 shallots, cut into fourths

2 oz/55 g dark chocolate, grated

salt and pepper

GARNISH

2 tbsp chopped fresh parsley

2 fresh bay leaves, optional

2 Preheat the oven to 400°F/200°C. Stir in 1¼ cups of the wine and all of the bouillon, and return the meat to the casserole. Add the thyme, bay leaf, juniper berries, cloves, and cinnamon, and season with salt and pepper. Bring to a boil, stirring, then cook in the oven for 1 hour. Top up the casserole with more wine from time to time, if necessary.

3 Meanwhile, make a cross in the bottom of each chestnut and transfer them to a cookie sheet. Bake at 400°F/200°C for 20 minutes, then shell them.

4 While the chestnuts are cooking, place the shallots in a small roasting

pan and coat them with the remaining oil. Roast at the same oven temperature for 15–20 minutes, until golden and tender.

5 Remove the casserole from the oven and lift out the meat with a slotted spoon. Place it in a serving dish, add the chestnuts and shallots, and keep warm. Strain the cooking juices into a clean pan. Discard the contents of the strainer. Set the pan over medium heat, bring to a boil, and cook until slightly reduced. Stir in the chocolate until melted, and adjust the seasoning if necessary. Pour the sauce over the meat, sprinkle with the parsley, and bay leaves if using, and serve.

1 Heat 3 tablespoons of the oil in a large, flameproof casserole. Add the veal and cook over medium heat, stirring, until lightly browned. Remove from the casserole and set aside. Add the onion, garlic, carrots, celery, and chiles to the casserole and cook, stirring, for 5 minutes, until the onion is softened.

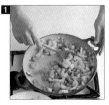

Layered Chocolate Mousse

Three layers of rich mousse give this elegant dessert extra chocolate appeal. It is a little fiddly to prepare, but well worth the extra effort.

3 hrs   10 mins

SERVES 4

INGREDIENTS

3 eggs

4 tbsp superfine sugar

1¼ cups milk

1 envelope gelatin

3 tbsp water

1¼ cups heavy cream

2¾ oz/75 g dark chocolate

2¾ oz/75 g white chocolate

2¾ oz/75 g light chocolate

chocolate caraque, to decorate
(see page 5)

1 Line a 1-lb/450-g loaf pan with baking parchment. Separate the eggs, putting each egg white in a separate bowl. Place the egg yolks and sugar in a large mixing bowl and whisk until well combined. Place the milk in a pan and heat gently, stirring, until almost boiling. Pour the milk onto the egg yolk mixture, whisking constantly.

2 Set the bowl over a pan of gently simmering water and cook, stirring, until the mixture thickens enough to thinly coat the back of a wooden spoon.

3 Sprinkle the gelatin over the water in a small heatproof bowl and let it go spongy. Place over a pan of hot water and stir until dissolved. Stir into the hot mixture. Let the mixture cool.

4 Whip the cream until just holding its shape. Fold into the egg custard, then divide the mixture equally among 3 bowls. Melt the 3 types of chocolate separately. Fold the dark chocolate into one egg custard portion. Whisk one egg white until standing in soft peaks and fold into the dark chocolate custard until combined.

Pour into the prepared pan and level the top. Chill in the coldest part of the refrigerator until just set. The remaining mixtures should stay at room temperature.

5 Fold the white chocolate into another portion of the egg custard. Whisk another egg white and fold in. Pour on top of the dark chocolate layer and chill quickly. Repeat with the remaining light chocolate and egg white. Chill for at least 2 hours, until set. To serve, carefully turn out onto a serving dish and decorate with chocolate caraque.

Chocolate Marquise

This classic French dish is part way between a mousse and a parfait. It is usually chilled in a large mold, but here it is made in individual molds.

2½ hrs   5 mins

SERVES 6

INGREDIENTS

7 oz/200 g dark chocolate

generous ⅓ cup butter

3 egg yolks

⅓ cup superfine sugar

1 tsp chocolate extract or 1 tbsp chocolate-flavored liqueur

1¼ cups heavy cream

TO SERVE

crème fraîche or thick plain yogurt

chocolate-dipped fruits

unsweetened cocoa, to dust

1 Break the chocolate into pieces. Place the chocolate and butter in a bowl over a pan of gently simmering water and stir until melted and well combined. Remove from the heat and let cool.

2 Place the egg yolks in a mixing bowl with the superfine sugar and whisk until pale and fluffy. Using an electric whisk running on low speed, slowly whisk in the cooled chocolate mixture. Stir in the chocolate extract or chocolate-flavored liqueur.

3 Whip the cream until just holding its shape. Fold it into the chocolate mixture. Spoon into 6 small custard pots or individual metal molds. Chill the desserts for at least 2 hours.

4 To serve, turn out the desserts onto individual serving dishes. If you have difficulty turning them out, dip the pots or molds into warm water for a few seconds to help the marquise to slip out. Serve with chocolate-dipped fruit, and crème fraîche or yogurt, and dust with cocoa.

COOK'S TIP

The slight tartness of the crème fraîche or yogurt contrasts well with this very rich dessert. Dip the fruit in white chocolate to give a good color contrast.

Rich Chocolate Ice Cream

A rich chocolate ice cream, delicious on its own or with chocolate sauce. For a special dessert, serve it in these attractive trellis cups.

4–5 hrs   12 mins

SERVES 6

INGREDIENTS

1 egg

3 egg yolks

scant ½ cup superfine sugar

1¼ cups whole milk

9 oz/250 g dark chocolate

1¼ cups heavy cream

TRELLIS CUPS

3½ oz/100 g dark chocolate

1 Beat together the egg, egg yolks, and superfine sugar in a mixing bowl, until well combined. Heat the milk until it is almost boiling.

2 Gradually pour the hot milk onto the eggs, whisking as you do so. Place the bowl over a pan of gently simmering water and cook, stirring, until the mixture thickens sufficiently to thinly coat the back of a wooden spoon.

3 Break the dark chocolate into small pieces and add to the hot custard. Stir until the chocolate has melted. Remove from the heat, cover with a sheet of dampened baking parchment, and let cool.

4 Whip the cream until just holding its shape, then fold into the cooled chocolate custard. Transfer to a freezer container and freeze for 1–2 hours, until the mixture is frozen 1 inch/2.5 cm from the sides.

5 Scrape the ice cream into a chilled bowl and beat again until smooth. Refreeze until firm.

6 To make the trellis cups, invert a 12-cup muffin pan and cover 6 alternate mounds with plastic wrap. Melt the chocolate, place it in a paper pastry bag, and snip off the end.

7 Pipe a circle around the bottom of a muffin-cup mound and repeat with the other 11 mounds. Then pipe chocolate back and forth over each mound to form a trellis; carefully pipe a double thickness. Pipe around the bottom again. Chill until set, then lift from the pan and remove the plastic wrap. Serve the ice cream in the trellis cups.

Mississippi Mud Pie

An all-time favorite with chocoholics—the "mud" refers to the gooey, rich chocolate layer of the cake.

🍮 3½ hrs   🕐 1 hr 10 mins

SERVES 8

INGREDIENTS

2 cups all-purpose flour

¼ cup unsweetened cocoa

⅔ cup butter

2 tbsp superfine sugar

about 2 tbsp cold water

FILLING

¾ cup butter

2⅓ cups dark brown sugar

4 eggs, lightly beaten

4 tbsp unsweetened cocoa, sifted

5½ oz/150 g dark chocolate

1¼ cups light cream

1 tsp chocolate extract

TO DECORATE

1¾ cups heavy cream, whipped

chocolate flakes, and quick chocolate curls (see page 5)

1 To make the pie dough, sift the flour and cocoa into a mixing bowl. Rub in the butter, until the mixture resembles fine bread crumbs. Stir in the sugar and enough cold water to mix to a soft dough. Chill for 15 minutes.

2 Roll out the dough on a lightly floured counter and use to line a deep 9-inch/23-cm loose-bottomed tart pan or ceramic tart dish. Line with foil or baking parchment and baking beans. Bake blind in a preheated oven, 375°F/190°C, for 15 minutes. Remove the beans, and foil or parchment, and then cook for another 10 minutes, until crisp.

3 To make the filling, beat the butter and sugar in a bowl and gradually beat in the eggs with the cocoa. Melt the chocolate (see page 5) and beat it into the mixture with the light cream and the chocolate extract.

4 Pour the mixture into the cooked pie shell and bake at 325°F/170°C for about 45 minutes, or until the filling is set.

5 Remove the mud pie from the oven and let cool completely, then transfer the pie to a serving plate, if preferred. Cover with the whipped cream and let chill.

6 Decorate the pie with quick chocolate curls and chocolate flakes and then let chill until ready to serve.

Triple Stripe Cream

Layers of chocolate, vanilla, and coffee, topped with a swirl of whipped cream or white chocolate caraque, make a simple but elegant dessert.

🐑 15 mins, plus 2 hrs chilling ⏱ 20 mins

SERVES 6

INGREDIENTS

1½ cups superfine sugar

6 tbsp cornstarch

3¼ cups milk

3 egg yolks

6 tbsp unsalted butter, diced

1 heaping tbsp instant coffee powder

2 tsp vanilla extract

2 tbsp unsweetened cocoa, sifted

⅔ cup whipped cream, or white chocolate caraque (see page 5), to decorate

1 Put ½ cup of the superfine sugar and 2 tablespoons of the cornstarch in a small, heavy-bottomed pan. Gradually, whisk in one-third of the milk. Set the pan over low heat and whisk in one of the egg yolks. Bring to a boil, whisking constantly, and boil for 1 minute. Remove the pan from the heat and stir in 1 tablespoon of the butter, and all the coffee powder. Set aside to cool slightly, then divide among 6 glasses and smooth the surfaces.

2 Place ½ cup of the remaining sugar and 2 tablespoons of the remaining cornstarch in a small, heavy-bottomed pan. Gradually, whisk in 1¼ cups of the remaining milk. Set the pan over low heat and whisk in one of the remaining egg yolks. Bring to a boil, whisking constantly, and boil for 1 minute. Remove the pan from the heat and stir in 2 tablespoons of the remaining butter, and all the vanilla. Set aside to cool slightly, then divide the vanilla mixture among the glasses and smooth the surfaces.

3 Put the remaining sugar and cornstarch in a small, heavy-bottomed pan. Gradually, whisk in the remaining milk. Set the pan over low heat and whisk in the last egg yolk. Bring to a boil, whisking constantly, and boil for 1 minute. Remove from the heat and stir in the remaining butter, and all the cocoa. Set the mixture aside to cool slightly, then divide among the glasses. Cover with plastic wrap and chill in the refrigerator for 2 hours, until set.

4 Whip the cream until thick, then pipe a swirl on top of each of the desserts. Alternatively, decorate with white chocolate caraque. Serve immediately.

Chocolate Boxes

Guests will think you have spent hours creating these little boxes, but a few tricks (such as ready-made cake) make them quick to put together.

20 mins, plus 1 hr chilling/setting   5 mins

SERVES 4

INGREDIENTS

8 oz/225 g dark chocolate

about 8 oz/225 g store-bought or ready-made plain or chocolate sponge cake

2 tbsp apricot jelly

⅔ cup heavy cream

1 tbsp maple syrup

3½ oz/100 g prepared fresh fruit, such as small strawberries, raspberries, kiwifruit, or red currants

1 Melt the dark chocolate (see page 5) and spread it evenly over a large sheet of baking parchment. Let set in a cool room.

2 When just set, cut the chocolate into 2-inch/5-cm squares and remove from the parchment. Make sure that your hands are as cool as possible and handle the chocolate as little as possible.

3 Cut the cake into 2 cubes, 2 inches/5 cm across, then cut each cube in half horizontally. Warm the apricot jelly and brush it over the sides of the cake pieces. Carefully press a chocolate square onto each side of the cake pieces to make 4 chocolate boxes with cake at the bottom. Chill in the refrigerator for 20 minutes.

4 Whip the heavy cream with the maple syrup until just holding its shape. Spoon or pipe a little of the mixture into each chocolate box.

5 Decorate the top of each box with the prepared fruit. If desired, the fruit can be partly dipped into melted chocolate and allowed to set before being placed into the boxes.

COOK'S TIP

For the best results, keep the chocolate boxes well chilled, and fill and decorate them just before you want to serve them.

Chocolate Butterfly Cakes

Filled with a tangy lemon cream, these appealing cakes will be a favorite with adults and children alike.

🄶 🄶 🄶

30 mins   🕐 15 mins

MAKES 12

INGREDIENTS

½ cup soft margarine

½ cup superfine sugar

1¼ cups self-rising flour

2 large eggs

2 tbsp unsweetened cocoa

1 oz/25 g dark chocolate, melted

LEMON BUTTER CREAM

generous ⅓ cup unsalted butter, softened

1⅓ cups confectioners' sugar, sifted

zest of ½ lemon, grated

1 tbsp lemon juice

confectioners' sugar, to dust

1 Place 12 individual paper cases in a shallow muffin pan. Place the margarine, superfine sugar, flour, eggs, and cocoa in a large mixing bowl and beat together with an electric whisk, until the mixture is just smooth. Beat in the melted chocolate.

2 Spoon equal amounts of the mixture into each paper case, filling them three-fourths full. Bake in a preheated

oven, 350°F/180°C, for 15 minutes, or until springy to the touch. Transfer to a wire rack and let cool.

3 Meanwhile, make the lemon butter cream. Place the butter in a mixing bowl and beat until fluffy, then gradually beat in the confectioners' sugar. Beat in the lemon zest and gradually add the lemon juice, beating well.

4 When cold, cut the top off each cake, using a serrated knife. Cut each cake top in half.

5 Spread or pipe the lemon butter cream over the cut surface of each cake and push the 2 cut pieces of cake top into the frosting to form butterfly wings. Sprinkle with confectioners' sugar.

VARIATION

For a chocolate butter cream, beat the butter and confectioners' sugar together, then beat in 1 oz/25 g melted dark chocolate.

Pain au Chocolat

These croissants can be a bit fiddly to make, but the layers of flaky pie dough enclosing a fabulous rich chocolate filling are worth the effort.

3¼ hrs   20–25 mins

MAKES 12

I N G R E D I E N T S

¾ cup butter, softened, plus extra for greasing

4 cups strong all-purpose flour

½ tsp salt

6 g sachet of rapid-rise dry yeast

2 tbsp shortening

1 egg, beaten lightly

1 cup lukewarm water

3½ oz/100 g dark chocolate, broken into 12 squares

beaten egg, to glaze

confectioners' sugar, to dust

1   Lightly grease a cookie sheet. Sift the flour and salt into a mixing bowl and stir in the yeast. Rub in the fat with your fingertips. Add the egg and enough of the water to mix to a soft dough. Knead for about 10 minutes to make a smooth elastic dough.

2   Roll out to form a 15 x 8-inch/ 38 x 20-cm rectangle. Divide the remaining butter into 3 portions. Dot one portion over two-thirds of the rectangle, leaving a small border around the edge.

3   Fold the rectangle into 3 by first folding the plain part of the dough over and then the other side. Seal the edges of the dough by pressing with a rolling pin. Give the dough a quarter turn so the sealed edges are at the top and bottom. Re-roll and fold (without adding butter), then wrap the dough and chill for 30 minutes.

4   Repeat steps 2 and 3 until all of the butter has been used, chilling the dough each time. Re-roll and fold twice more without butter. Chill for a final 30 minutes.

5   Roll the dough to an 18 x 12-inch/ 46 x 30-cm rectangle, then trim and halve lengthwise. Cut each half into 6 rectangles and brush with beaten egg.

6   Place a chocolate square at one end of each rectangle and roll up to form a sausage. Press the ends together and place, seam-side down, on the cookie sheet. Cover and let rise for 40 minutes in a warm place. Brush with beaten egg and bake in a preheated oven, 425°F/220°C, for 20–25 minutes, until golden. Cool on a wire rack. Dust with confectioners' sugar and serve warm or cold.

Chocolate Wheatmeals

A good everyday cookie, these wheatmeals will keep well in an airtight container for at least 1 week. Dip them in white, light, or dark chocolate.

1 hr   15–20 mins

MAKES 20

INGREDIENTS

⅓ cup butter, plus extra for greasing

⅔ cup raw brown sugar

1 egg

1 oz/25 g wheatgerm

1 cup whole-wheat self-rising flour

½ cup white self-rising flour, sifted

4½ oz/125 g chocolate

1 Lightly grease a cookie sheet. Beat the remaining butter with the sugar until fluffy. Add the egg and beat well. Stir in the wheatgerm and flours. Bring the mixture together with your hands.

2 Roll rounded teaspoonfuls of the mixture into balls and place on the prepared cookie sheet, allowing room for the cookies to expand during cooking.

3 Flatten the cookies slightly with the prongs of a fork. Bake in a preheated oven, 350°F/180°C, for 15–20 minutes,

until golden. Remove from the oven and let cool on the cookie sheet for a few minutes before transferring to a wire rack to cool completely.

4 Melt the chocolate, then dip each cookie in the chocolate to cover the

flat side and come a little way around the edges. Let the excess chocolate drip back into the bowl.

5 Place the cookies on a sheet of baking parchment and let the chocolate set in a cool place before serving.

COOK'S TIP

These cookies can be frozen very successfully. Freeze them at the end of Step 3 for up to 3 months. Thaw and then dip them in melted chocolate.